Love Garden at the End of the World

by Christine Stephens-Krieger

Praise for *Love Garden at the End of the World*:

"There is talent and energy here, and hard-earned truth. Christine Stephens-Krieger's poems are exuberant and effusive in their physicality, a celebration of childhood, motherhood, of violets and clavicles, heartache and joy, the human, animal/vegetable surrealism of everyday life."

—Dan Gerber, author of *Sailing through Cassiopeia* and *A Primer on Parallel Lives*

"Christine Stephens-Krieger's debut volume of poetry *Love Garden at the End of the World* is a richly mythic, sensual and feminist exploration of womanhood. Readers will recognize and thrill with the West Michigan landscape and with lush descriptions of the natural world. The whole book is steeped in the landscape of Michigan's dunes and lakes. There are many pleasures for readers—especially Christine Stephens-Krieger's wide open stance embracing life, adventure, and especially love and relationships. Her writing is best when it surprises us, as with a line like 'Time is a grenade in the chest / with the pin pulled at birth.' This is a book of becoming, of growing, just like gardens grow. Some of the most memorable poems here are ones about her father, several love poems, and others that wrestle with the concept of death, especially 'The Art of Death' and a late one in the volume called 'Last Will and Testament.' I look forward to the path of Christine Stephens-Krieger's poetry in the future and am confident other readers will want to follow her as well."

—Patricia Clark, author of *O Lucky Day* and *Self-Portrait with a Million Dollars*

"Christine Stephens-Krieger writes of a child's thrilling sense of the fullness of her being and of the beauty and power of mature love. In her nuanced, skillfully wrought, and compelling poems, she pays close attention to our daily common risks while vividly portraying creative mystery, adult vulnerability, and the paradoxes we live with: the 'secret no one knows / the same one everyone knows.'"

—Lee Upton, author of *Wrongful* and *The Day Every Day Is*

"This book is a miracle of poetics and a testament to what can be said when poetics truly, effectively, actually express the human heart's passion. I've learned more about love from reading this book, and there's no greater gift than that. It is so brave in its vulnerability. This book is a true gardener's guide for the greatest kind of thing we can grow as human beings. I can't wait 'til I can buy a copy and share these poems with others in my life. I feel blessed to have read them and I'm thankful for their light."

—Neil Kaufman, author of *Jungle Gyms for Monkey Minds*

"The poems of Christine Stephens-Krieger explore the little *everything* that makes up each passing moment, its nuance and flavors, blue slag glass retrieved from a lake, onion trucks and giant windmills, kids playing statues, tomatoes just off the vine. Lovers holding hands 'in a rainy cemetery.' The body going about its own mysterious changes. Nothing stands still; these poems honor and cherish how, on a daily basis, in grief and in love, we too keep on going: 'We're rich with cargo. We travel.'"

—Nancy Eimers, author of *Oz, A Grammar to Waking, No Moon,* and *Destroying Angel*

Cover image by the poet.
Author photo credit: Jesselyn Zbytowski Photography

ISBN: 978-1-968226-00-8

Published by Grand River Poetry Press. Grand Rapids, MI
grandriverpoetrycollective.com

This book is dedicated to friends gone too soon, and friends still with me.

with love and gratitude for my mom and dad...

and as always, for Scott.

Table of Contents

"At the center of everything we call 'the arts,'
and children call 'play,' is something
which seems somehow alive."
　　—*Lynda Barry*

"You only have to let the soft animal of your body
　　　　love what it loves. ..."
　　—*Mary Oliver*

"When I realized the storm
was inevitable, I made it
my medicine. ..."
　　—*Andrea Gibson*

Part 1

Incarnation

Time is a grenade in the chest
with the pin pulled at birth.

Darkness is standard,
illumination optional.

The room smells mineral,
smells like water lines

and words like *cistern,*
cavern, clam, clamber.

Would I disturb this
stillness with a pebble,

a message from the world above?
I swallow, hold myself tight

to the precipice edge,
pebble ready, listening.

Everything is Magic

No one is out. Only me.
    Late summer,
long shadows, morning dusk.

No one cares. Only me.
    My bike is the best bike.
Everything is the same color as me,

twilight limned in gold,
    rose and olive ochre,
sure there's something new

around the corner, sure
    the message is for me,
sure of joy. The wind

is a little cool whirling
    behind me in tiny hurricanes,
turbulence in my wake.

The Secret Everyone Knows

Once, I drowned.
Once, I died for a minute
in the arms of the octopus
at the bottom of the lake.

This memory, this moment,
seared. I'm wearing
blue and white gingham
with white eyelet fringe.

My bangs are crooked.
My cousins laugh, say,
Ma cut yer bangs, huh?
It's a family reunion.

Once the world came into focus.
Once, my body
was a different place.
Somewhere inside me,

that lake is still alive
with the octopus reaching for me
from the bottom. It was
real and not real, but *real.*

All of it, I know.
I recognize everything
like a dream of a place
I've never been before.

Lungs full of water, I sink down
into Death's sunless depths;
I know nothing of fear,
my body never learned it.

Spun to perfection,
I'm a diamond held tight
in the endless grip
of my new old friend.

Though they pull me to the surface,
flush water from my lungs
and pray for me under the hard sky,
I will never be the same child.

I have a secret no one knows,
the same one everyone knows,
though everyone tells me to hush.
It's over now, they say. *Hush, hush.*

Myth of the Perfect Girl

I reached perfection at age twelve,
but no one noticed. Perfection

happens everywhere, all
the time not knowing itself,

perfect like dirt, like a squid,
perfection under wraps, enspelled,

swapped with changelings,
forced to live a goblin life,

hidden under veils, sometimes buried,
too precious, thrown in a pond to keep,

treasure only worth its legend,
perfect glimmer in the dark.

Once, I was every saint,
had a map for every step.

I bought the magic, bookworm amateur
armed with a pen and a timid knock.

Perfect, I watched others transform,
fall into ruin when they ate the magic beans.

I watched for the color change, texture
shift, the red marks and wild glances,

the smirking and escaping, the finding
a million ways to break their shells.

When I was perfect, adulthood
was the land of broken dreams.

A witness, I swore to never get fat,
never have kids, never marry.

Perfect, I signed my name on every page
through my *School Days* book… perfect,

I saw no reason I would change.
Perfect black and white shapes

cast perfect shadows, make perfect sense.
I tell myself, I'll never make that face, never

eat the whole cake, won't wear that, will not—
but then make the face, eat the cake, wear the dress,

those shoes, get in the car, go for the ride. Fall.
Perfect falling. Petals descend just so.

The Queen of Childhood

When childhood
lost its queen,

everyone was sad
to see me go.

My light faded
from the scene.

Outside,
monsters.

They spun us round,
made statues of us.

One after another,
we were called.

Still Life

I knew she was gone for good when I climbed
the spiral stairs to her room and found spiny
paint brushes poking out of mayonnaise jars,
her rows of turpentine and red wine left behind.

Father hated that attic silence, her blue smock,
all the unfinished portraits of me.
I used to sit in the posing chair, stare at them,
and wonder what was so impossible about my eyebrows,

the bones in my nose, my unremarkable chin.
She left all twelve canvases, her favorite
fan brushes, her best tubes of color.
Now I imagine her outside where color is real:

she stands in the street with her suitcase,
the moon casting a blue shadow,
the evening gray and brown.
As she waits, the headlights

of her lover's car will splash her dress so white
she'll be blinded till she's miles away.

Icarus as a Girl

As my mother's daughter, I had choices.
Doors opened where luck would have it,
a least resistance path, each step revealing
the step ahead. Fate was a crazy game
we played with the gods, trust just an idea,

but I knew I was meant for more,
meant for bigger things… I was born to give it all away.
I had choices but never tried to escape.
It never came up in conversation.
Babyfat, summer freckles, beach blond,

sleeping cheek bones, clavicles folded like angel wings.
My memory is fishy and warped, but if I know this girl,
she'd wear her wings high over her head
like they want to fly and she can't keep them down.
Girl like this wants to see how high she can go.

Girl falls for the sake of falling.

The Enlightenment of Eve

The endless ways, the days and nights,
secret shakes, coded notes, smoking
behind the shed, the specific details

of fornication left out of movie scenes,
hidden under covers, hinted in books,
song lyrics, surveyed in prayer, spread

in magazine pages hidden under rocks,
photos that disgraced the rain and left
more questions than they answered, and

Mother Earth, please tell me: What does
virgin mean? At what point will I know?
When may I eat the apple? And when I eat

the apple, will knowing just fall onto me?
Will there be new monsters to battle? Will
knowing mean throwing everything else away?

Or does knowing unveil new patterns in the canopy?
At what point should I abandon the blueprints,
assemble by feel in the dark, just wing it?

But the world only shrugs and rolls over, and I'm
born once again into a bigger room, broken in,
tanned and softened, a looser grip on the details.

The breaking was easy but spectacular, like
heroes to crucify and fools who lose everything
that possessed them on the way down.

Drunk Ages

I walked around like that all night,
 and no one told me.
Morning broke the news, broke my head, my dress

a crumpled wreck of cigarette burns
 I found
on the closet floor. They called me crazy,

called me slut, and no one told me.
 My body knew
but didn't tell me. Wherever I went, no one knew me.

They saw but didn't see. They kicked me out
 of their houses.
They said, *la la la la la la la la.*

Dawn was a gift I didn't want to deserve,
 but time marches over,
time rolls, time crushes, and bears it all.

Mother

Mother is silent, mother weeps, mother sighs.
Mother does the difficult thing. All the grand
mothers know sacrifice is required. Silence
mothers all darkness. Mother knits and kneads,
mother rises early. Something inside her must
mother at all times, the holding, clapping, shouting
mothers in the rain, cups of wine, fresh bread only
mothers can make. Mother falls away and comes back.
Mother hides to make her own stories, her cave walls
mother every darkness, passed on to me. Inherit the
mother, become the mother, swallow the darkness.

Mother, you know what I must do, how I must fall.
Mother, you watch, sister who made me, carried me,
mothered me from afar and up close the way every
mother must release an entire skein of life to the wind,
mother of all invisible fingers ruffling tree tops,
mother of storms, faster and faster flowing away,
mother who watches and steps aside and watches,
mother who knows I must learn my own truths,
mother who knew about monsters and said nothing,
mother, maker of the silver ladder we climb to heavenly
Mother of god, we contain mountains, multitudes,

mother of pearl glancing invisible colors seen by crowds
mother never dreamed of, hubbubs and nuisances. The grand
mothers rule, they outnumber us, tell us what to do,
motherly swords the world has never seen. I can hear the
mothers sing, scream, tell stories, antidotes,
motherly love, the kind you don't know about until you
mother another, release another version of yourself to
mother more perhaps. Instinct takes over. No control.
Mother says, *Strike fast, play the chances, take hearts.*
Mother obeys. She only speaks from experience. Her own
mothers whisper: anything to survive, anything for more.

The Ascension of Joy

Stellar wind, stellar wind,
what does it mean to be a woman?

Some things don't change. When
I'm joyful, I'm precious. Sometimes,

occasionally, every now and then,
joy finds the same child.

Joy drops in... once on a street
outside a bookstore, once on my bike,

once while swinging, once six months
pregnant with a stowaway in a car

with a man who never touched me or said
a forward thing but was kind and drove

us down a late summer lane of dappled
shades: olive and ochre, subdued violets

with a hint of fall... for no reason then,
all the life inside me leapt up.

Renovation

She lines the walls with red velvet curtains,
barricades the door with her body,
protecting herself from me, her mother.

She's a sandbag dropped from a hot air balloon
and makes herself comfortable in her fist-sized
apartment, bulldozes the neighborhood to stretch

her legs. I'm certain she'll shrug me off
like a loose garment, step out of me,
then borrow my make-up and clothes.

She's growing into the shape of me,
will someday be a woman
incapable of killing so small a thing,

who ignores clashing wall paper patterns,
swelled breasts, a flattened bladder. Or what if
it's a boy, muscling his way around,

impatiently awaiting his big debut.
He shimmies his feet and taps his fingers
along my spine. He orders room service,

pulls my craving strings: *Send more
broccoli and chocolate*, charging the bill to me,
his mother. We're both waiting

for his father to love him, to hum his
absent-minded songs through my skin's speakers
and animate his mute world. My son

would know his father's hands if they'd caress
my belly, so like his hands on the inside.
It'll be a cinch once he's out, little man,

little mirror, crazy hair, crooked feet.
The conspiracy's complete. I can feel
him just below my skin, moving things around,

already planning, ready to kick.

Bloodstone and Agate

Can you see my fingers think as they braid my hair
before I reach for scissors?
They'll tell you about the hottest summer,

my pregnancy slowing my walks
in a city only bearable at night, tell you
my body knew what to do

the first time we made love and later,
how to push our son into your hands,
my forehead's vessels bursting like fireworks.

I used to imagine those lights on a string around my neck,
the fragile stalks of snapdragons—
things we can never save, like desire

on a hundred degree day or the time
my hands flew white through a letter I found,
a love letter to another woman.

I wish I knew more about rage or forgiveness,
wish I could erase the marks from my skin,
lift my breasts above time and our child's thirst.

I paint my nails, clip my hair, slip lace over my skin,
and still, those first afternoons we shook the house
are gone for good. If I could, I'd keep you in a shoe box

rattling with bloodstone and agate
I gathered at a lake's edge. Not even the stars
dazzled like those wet stones in the sun,

not your words last night on the porch as I lit a match,
sending bits of letter spiraling up the sky
burning through my singed fingers.

Sleeping Beauty Awakens

What wakes me?
My head perks in the dark.
My neck breaks in the dark.

The wind blows through the dark.
How did I get here?
On the floor in a room so dark

I must've gone blind.
I have to touch my eyes
to know they're open.

I'm tucked in like a diver,
only I'm on my side, curled tight.
I fell asleep like this,

left like this in the dark.
I have to break my back to get up.
Stones break the length of my spine,

trees root and twine down my mountain,
pierce my liver, wrap my lips
and clavicles, my hips and sternum.

They pull me in, tuck me under,
root me in place,
cover my mouth, cringe me,

press me, shut me, keep me
until I'm a Greek myth,
a fairytale with dubious moral.

Leaves sprout from my fingertips.
My arms become birch bones
lost in stacks of white bracelets.

I forget my face, my voice, my name.
The night I slept in a ball
so tight my neck broke,

one night lasted a thousand nights.
I woke old, haggard, bent, lost,
hedgerows grown round me, mazes

of thorns and florid blossoms.
Many ages will pass before
I stand up straight again.

New Girl in Paradise

Collar bones, clavicles, *clavicles!*
Once sung like a favorite word,
once swan wings, my clavicles

were Nike flips, whirlwinds
on bike rides, cool mornings
before shadows gave up the street.

When I rode my bike in the sun,
that banana seat sparkled like a million
purple diamonds between my legs,

super girl with dare-devil clavicles,
whole new universes born
in the hollows of my collar bones,

teardrop slips of wind spinning
windows into new dimensions.
The day opens for this girl. I wear her

like a flag, a pennant for a battle
where darkness owns every outcome.
Here is an animal who will take a ride.

I've forgotten her name in fairy tales
where they break the girl to pieces
and she scatters like a murder of crows.

Monsters steal her knives and clubs
only to knife and club her with them.
She gives away all her treasures,

her glow in the dark brontosaurus,
her bronze medal for winning, her damn heart
which returns sometimes like a skipping stone,

sometimes on fire, often in a green cloak.
Each time her clavicles sink deeper,
hunch under their grip of flesh,

the lost clavicles of girldom. Now,
I remake my body in search of collar bones.
I miss those lost dimensions.

Part 2

Becoming Someone New

To become someone new I re-invent my bones.
My spine is a circus act:

I'm a stack of spinning plates on a stick!
My vertebrae make an expert game of Jenga.

My body is an animal dreaming
while my mind is the architect of doom.

To become someone new, I transubstantiate:
I think I am, I know I am, I am!

My body is a parade float—
my mind says this isn't happening.

To become someone new,
I give myself to monsters.

I mean nothing to me. I can remake myself,
rig an apparatus with dowels and duct tape,

purple rubber bands saved from asparagus,
blue from broccoli… I'm close to the real deal!

To become someone new, I escape via train windows,
leave this tundra in search of softer ground.

I was born a marigold seed, one end dipped in ink,
the other a yellow parachute,

born a clever wind, born a god, a servant,
a lover, and a love.

Chosen, plucked, tadpole seed, falling
star, I was born to become someone new.

I hurricane, tsunami, and erupt.
I avalanche and earthquake.

My villagers run screaming!
I'm becoming someone new,

still waking, still waking up,
feeling the pull of a yawn and then yawning.

The tickers record, cliffs fall into the sea.
Glaciers scrape, boulders dance,

all into the sea. Body says:
What time is it? Where am I? What is my name?

Time flows at rock speed. Trolls converse.
From down here, it sounds like thunder.

I grow mute and full of words.
The quieter I am, the more I have to say.

How to See the Invisible World

1

Giant silver industrial chimney
shimmers the sky like a jet engine
beside the highway where the back

of a red pickup truck
spins a vortex of dead leaves into a confetti
whirlwind within its wake

while in the middle distance eight hot air balloons
climb the air like bubbles through water
racing each other to the surface.

2

A plume of white steam climbs the sky,
a giant exclamation mark declaring something
that drifts into a flock of seagulls and mare's tails

amidst tiers of clouds that depict a dragon, a fish
and then scatter into waves that reveal
the topography of the sky, those mountains and valleys,

those castles and impossible cities
only seen when something is dancing in it,
the way snow reveals the shape of the wind

and clouds reveal the sea above me. Birds climb the air
like swimmers doing the butterfly whose arms swirl round
and round through the thick air. We call it flying.

3

Today we're driving three hours North to visit ruins
abandoned in mystery, full of ghosts and haunted stones

someone placed there and left thousands of years ago,
like skipping moments skittering across time
that is always flowing all around and through us.

Invisible eddies curlicue into fractals
that iterate endlessly in this pool of spacetime where we swim,
what we call "now." Together we move through the world.

4

We fit together like a dragon and a fish in the sky
as far away as death seems to be, you know,
not the next thing or the thing after that,

but so close and so far away
I have to throw myself into the wind to see it,
my hair gone wild and white, my body a parody,

a less than graceful silhouette—beautiful nonetheless,
hands clasped with another lost cloud
in a world so fluid, nothing is lost. We drift together

toward our demise, but in the meantime
we dance in the wind, gather stones and pebbles,
build mountains and monuments. We swim upstream

and down. We do our very best for a moment
to hover in place, to be still, to be silent.
We find a rich place to drop our roots

where the soil is teeming with life
to feed our bodies while our hearts thrive
in the invisible. Like love, it's everything.

What's Important

Since the only thing we can be sure of is the abyss,
write your poems in stone and whisper them to someone,
make them promise not to tell, *it's a secret.*

Because the asteroid will one day plunge us all into darkness,
shout your poems from rooftops, sing them, howl them
so they echo long into the endless night.

Because the oceans will one day sizzle away,
make poems full of rain and storms that spatter and drench;
record the pleasure of immersion in water, the warm body hug.

So that we may carry on through dark days,
store poems like apples and potatoes in the cellar,
like seeds and bulbs and a big jar of honey.

Since you never know what tomorrow will bring,
take a moment to memorize the light
so one day you can tell a story about light.

When the sun's gone plasma and our planet
is on fire, call it death, call it what you will…
it's important to focus on the small things.

When everything changes irrevocably,
have a fallback moment so well memorized
you could spend your afterlife there.

Make it a good one, like a daydream you wander into
one afternoon blinded by a golden slant of sun
and the buzz of the bees in the flax and sunflowers

so you have to shake yourself awake
and you wonder how much time has passed
and from where you've just returned.

A Story About Light

Once I lay naked
in the arms of a lover
beneath the full bare sun

that covered us like a blanket,
touched us everywhere all at once,
primordial, quickening, and true.

For a moment, bathed in this light
I found myself erased,
blinded in a white out

within the ecstasy of entanglement.
Though I knew myself to be
corporeal, flesh and blood, human,

the part of me that's made of light
blurred to become one with the light,
warm and electric like waking from sleep,

like when you're touched by a god,
the flash of being burned by a fire
though it's millions of miles away

and still, the incandescence—
like all the light inside me
could blind a dark room,

like all the light inside me
amounts to the sun itself
or a distant star that lights the night.

Moments for My Father

I'd never seen a person
vacate a body before,
though I should not have been surprised
after the years, months, weeks, days, hours,

moments of watching him slip away,
bit by bit to the other side
with his brown eyes getting so big
in his skinny face, big and sad,

trying to say all the words
he never said in his life
like he'd been working on this tumor,
this tangle of words they cut out

his whole life. All the times
he should have said *I love you,*
all the times he should have said,
I love you, too. All the times

he shored up, he stowed away
moments like crystals embedded
in his mind, moments he swore
he would never forget.

Now it's up to me to bear witness.
When he died for a minute mid-surgery,
an angel told him he had to go back to earth.
I think he came back for me.

In that extra two and a half years,
we got ice cream and China Buffet
and I watched him slip away just as
I was getting to know him. But in that time

he forgot he didn't like to hold hands.
How often did I hear, "Love you, too, kiddo"?
And when I took him to see his brother,
he spoke easily, said it plain as day,

"It's your brother, your brother. I love you, man.
I love you," with the two of them just
holding onto each other and crying
like the sweetest little children.

What Went into the Seed

The sky of every day and
the moon that enlivens the night,
each nuance, each flavor.

The herbal path,
the carnal tug,
every time the world

exploded and reformed,
the long labors devoted
to creation and destruction.

If everything is natural,
then I must be, too,
and the things I create

like this poem, a seed,
a profound structure
that encapsulates me.

When our seeds collide:
a new universe bursts
into being, a new dance

of bees and butterflies
and the seeds
they leave behind

deep in the earth
fighting their way
like poems to the light.

Live Like Trees

Feel the heartbeat slow to root pulse,
the electric quiver of soil at its slowest,

the imperceptible slag of xylem
through the veins, flowing slower

than stars across the sky.
The world's in such a hurry, love.

The tree knows a child as a blur
and the automobile only by its smell.

Speed becomes invisible.
If I could move my arm as slowly

across this panorama of grass,
fallen leaves, the inevitable snow and sleep,

how many lifetimes could we spend together
inching into each other

over the years until we melt into an eternal kiss.
Each secret of the universe unravels

as thoughts inhabit moments as huge
as the earth in its lumberous play.

The true motion and hue of love passes
through a gigantic and slumbering heart.

Preparing to Leave

I have to trick myself into doing it,
pretend like I'm just doing the laundry,
the fridge needed cleaning anyway,

the lights set to timers almost without me looking.
All the bedding's clean and laundry done
and kitchen put away for our return,

our cats already pining for us at the cat hotel.
It'll only be a week for us but forever for them
wondering if we'll ever come back.

We hand our lives over to the airline,
plug ourselves into that machine
until delivered to the other side.

But now, the sun is playing with my knee
as I sit mostly under the umbrella
in the garden of my home pretending

none of this is really happening, I guess
a little fugue state I play in my brain
like a Bach record to help me endure

difficult things, like the time we got bad news,
sister's crying, but I piped up! Said it'll be okay.
We can do this together. And she—

she looks at me like she's worried I'm an idiot,
and maybe I am, asks if I did not understand
what the doctor said, but I'm already ten steps ahead.

It'll probably take me 10 years to unpack this moment,
but at the time I'm like:
this moment needs a positive note!

Let's save despair for later. It will come on its own
in spite of our plans or hopes or dreams,
says the handy dandy little fugue state....

Travel is not nearly as bad as my dad's brain cancer
turned out to be... or not usually—
and we'll only be gone a week

as opposed to the 2.5+ years of dad's cancer
and the 5+ years since his death now.
He was certainly not prepared to leave.

Even now, he seeps into my travel plans.
We are leaving now to visit my husband's father,
not my own, though mine should still be here.

Preparing to leave is like learning how to fly:
part faith, part hope, part fairy dust.
I close my eyes and imagine the world,

the safe flight, the meaningful visit, the return home
to our kitchen and our cats, who are so happy to see us
they can hardly believe just a few hours before

their hearts were broken into a million pieces
as they cried themselves to sleep every night
thinking we'd abandoned them. See?

This is why I don't think. Every thought seems to
slide down its own cyclone of fear as if to tell me
there's no way easy way to get ready to go.

Childhood Memory

On the picnic table in my backyard
under a night sky so deep and dark

I was determined to sleep under it
so I could think about infinity,

I never felt small before such vastness
but large, rather, huge, humungous!

Look at me, I remember thinking,
I am the universe thinking about the universe.

Leland Blues
—for Pam

Set in the shade of a weathered cross
bearing the name Yahtzee,
my friend leaves a flat, round stone.

I'm thinking the dog's owner
must have loved to shout it, *Yahtzee!*
Yahtzee! though the beach now rocks

the shore with silence for the dog
whose ashes scatter here. My friend
leaves the stone as a gesture,

a sacrifice of a keeper
recently scrutinized down
to just a few to take home,

each chosen by standards
strange until explained:
"This one because it's flat,"

she says over a palmful
of typical beach fare.
"This one because look,"

she points: "a peace sign,"
and then I see why
they're beautiful.

Waves stretch beyond
the horizon, our toes sunk
into a million pebbles

tumbled by the surf's pull
and push, every other detail
a blur along this big lake shore

weekend away with friends. Drunk
with the lake and giddy lighthouse
visions of horizons lost,

our pockets sunk
with petoskey and granite,
quartz and limestone,

dripping with fossils
the waves would inevitably tumble
to nothing anyway. Tiny, bright

blue bits wink in the surf,
a blue so blue the sky
must have fallen here, Leland blue

they call it, mellifluous name,
lost and found here, like Yahtzee
and my quest for treasure.

I search for more blue
while my friend speaks
to every dog we meet,

tells me about all the dogs
at the lodge and their ailments
and how hard it is to know

when it's time to let go.
Dogs parade through her life
with one name, *Katie, Our Katie,*

spoken like a saint's name,
or a lost child, or when the child
is us and we're the one left behind.

We shouldn't have to let go
of love like that. The way
grief can turn love into pain

can make us think we should stop,
but love tells us the only choice
is to hang on, to weather through,

to keep on loving. When they dumped
blue slag into Leland harbor
100 years ago, it was garbage.

Now my friend sees it, says,
"bits of beauty everywhere."
Before we leave the beach,

I get a look at the stone she left
for Yahtzee. I see two crinoid discs
in the flat, round limestone,

"Two eyes," she points out,
atop a long arm of cladopora
in a downward-shaped arch:

"… and a sad mouth," she adds.
She doesn't need to know
the corals drowned in mud

in the Devonian Age and
needed 400 million years
to be beautiful again. Maybe

that's how long the earth needs
to transform grief, to finally
be free of it. Or you can do

what my friend did. In an instant,
she made her sadness beautiful,
then she gave it away.

The Art of Death

Some suspect Death is cold,
but Death's kiss sears.

The rest of us wrestle in the grass like teenagers,
roll down dunes into the water below.

Electrified by the sky, we bite
the green and shred it with our teeth,

we rend the red and gnash it down,
we paw each other with hot hands.

Sugar-burned, full of photons,
eyes full of everything, spices

from a thousand miles away
dancing on our tongues

this body to feed and pad about,
these feet that slap the ground

all just dumb show and shadow,
all hollow and full of echoes.

No need to fear the final embrace.
It's everything you ever dreamed.

This Collection of Senses

How like a river are we, how like a flag,
an exclamation mark, cumulo nimbus,
how like a balloon are we always bursting
somewhere into the greater atmosphere,
always wafting back to the world

once again a member of the ocean.
Are we not party balloons filled with helium
on the very cusp of forever? Aren't we also
handfuls of confetti thrown into the wind,
and aren't we also the wind?

A mad scientist's contraption of delights,
Hello! No one knows how it works,
part velvet, part gristle, part fairy dust,
we have somehow enlivened the clay
with ancient and potent words

spoken into her intervals, the gaps left
with the sole purpose of developing
a little mystery of her own. In the dark
spaces between thought and intention
lies the mystery: What is life?

For what purpose am I contained
in this biomechanical rhythmic thumping
which happens to be my heart,
my own drum pounding me like a nail
into the earth one beat at a time?

What We Carry

What should we bring with us
to the End of the World?

I will carry these cats on my back
until they learn to walk beside me.

They will teach me to hunt, and
I will teach them to eat their kill.

I will carry this ukulele and this guitar
slung by leather bands to my shoulders

so that I can go on singing songs
about the End of the World.

I will carry pen, ink, and paper—
the better to fight the patriarchy.

Anything else I will smash
before I let it slow me down.

Love, you're coming, yes?
I'll drop everything to carry you.

Part 3

Love Garden at the End of the World

The love garden at the end of the world is shored up
against a narrow paved alley that connects
a block's worth of backyards and where we plant
our anniversary garden every year. Sunflowers'
spiral gathering of single blossoms tangle together
in the square dance we call our life together
here on this hill at the top of the world—
where on earth could be better than this?

The love garden at the end of the world is fenced in,
but the fence is flimsy and broken, the gate
unloved and hanging by a black iron hinge.
We bungee cord the gate shut
though it's wide enough to fit a cat through,
or a possum or groundhog or a wild turkey
as has recently been witnessed.

Cultivation of the love garden at the end of the world is easy.
We don't have weeds because we love dandelions.
Every year, a rogue band of yellow finches
eats all our echinacea, and the bluejays
squirrel away the black sunflower seeds.
Every year the rabbits gnaw
the umbrella of lacy kale down to a nub,
how far down determined by the depth of snow that year
and why we leave the garden untouched till Spring.

The love garden at the end of the world
gives new life to old Valentines,
pink plastic hearts on sticks
once in bouquets of roses
now in a bigger bouquet
proclaiming love, love, love
all the live long day.

For a moment, summer rises from my memory
like every past and future summer blended
together in an ocean of greenery,
lush life that will not be denied,
flowering, flowering, reaching vines,
for more flowering until we're covered,
eaten, swallowed. It's easy to assume
there will always be another summer,
but the love garden at the end of the world
assumes nothing and therefore celebrates
each tiny substantial thing.

Our First Spring

You were the one who lifted our feet
over and beyond the baby sparrow
whose mottled spots blended with earth
the way life blends with death, the way

fingers intertwine with fingers
as blades of feathers with wings of grass,
mixing blood with earth, transformed
into potential yet to test the air together. Now

this is our first night as husband and wife,
holding hands in a rainy cemetery in Spring
with all of heaven sprinkling its blessed drops
onto our heads, on tombstones, on fledgling wings.

In a place of death, we found life just beginning,
well hidden and one day ready to fly.

Dreaming Our Life

We've never lived this close to roses
or witnessed their spider deaths,
brown tendrils curling in.
Before they lost their yellow robes,

their voices woke us loud with scent,
as if they knew beauty transient,
jealous and nodding outside our window.
We understand this grasp for the moment,

both of us arriving here with boxes of words
to preserve our fading separate pasts
parceled out across a page.
Awake, our skin divides us,

and the roses transmit separate
messages inside our skulls
when only moments before,
our hands spoke in sleep and met

across a table in a Paris Cafe.
The velvet mettle clamored around us
when suddenly rain cast its net
and a man made a newspaper hat,

the headline reading *War!*
No matter how we laughed,
fear blurred our edges
when the silver dollops of rain

changed to asphalt
and we crumbled like wet soil
taking as long to fall
as an eyelid to bloom on morning.

My love, I swear I'll never leave you
so long as we mingle in the dirt
to feed the flowers,
the only beautiful aftermath of destruction.

The Natural History of All Enigmas

*"I came to know through his mouth
the natural history of all enigmas."*
—*Pablo Neruda*

I came for the green light,
the October moon,

his desire for the Latin of trees,
the force that sculpts sandstone cliffs,

trigonometry's spin,
the art of climbing,

the ancient ways we remember
the grit of existence.

I came away and floundered,
my hands open as stars,

my feet lessons in chaos:
I reeled against the world.

To connect is to twist the sheets,
spin by the elbow's crook,

bite a ripe plum, witness
the tapestry's map, genuflect.

The click and tong of an oud string,
the line and pigment,

the animating principle,
the finger's groan,

the acorn and oak,
razors and hammers,

the thunder's voice,
the serpent root,

Allahoo!
the tongue is a spoon,

the long way down,
the vine and its victim.

He told me once, *Half the trick*
is learning how to land.

His hands are open, his feet light,
a storm's at his back.

Thus we meet in the world,
we two,

the natural history
of all enigmas:

through earth's grain,
sky's ladder,

love's dark,
himself and myself as one.

Our Moment

This moment right now with all its stars,
     dirt, flowers, cats, all the birds,
         this whole house, all our air
             and gravity and today
                  contained here for us

Everything grows everywhere the way
     a vine fractals through space
         traces geometries, urged by love
             our moment kaleidoscopes
             through us

Within this moment
     we are rich in forget-me-nots
         we dig, we unearth, we build, we bury
         we feed the earth and
             the earth feeds us

Capture this moment for me
     in a butterfly net
         and kisses down my neck
             and by staring eternity
                  in the face for hours

How can this moment end but in tumbling
     a predictable arc but surprising nonetheless
         our love, this moment, familiar
             the way robins warble at our window
               as if they know us

Rock, Dreams, Air

1

The cliff in my throat teeters overhead,
wind and water etch away the consonants.

We walk through pure vowel, mockingbird.
Angel shale snaps like glottal stops.

Loose the wind from your feathers
like a thing searching for its word.

Kick a stone from the path. We'll
follow it on an otherwise bloodless plain.

2

I want to wreck our lives,
spill out of the lines,

run our colors together,
shale into schist,

I want everything with you.
I want to be terrified and austere.

Unfold the cloth from your chest, make it our map.
Anywhere is what I want with you.

3

I am sitting in the earth's mouth.
You are eating the horizon.
Stone swallows sun.

You are an outcrop, medusa's lost hero,
erosive, craggy, a deathwish, a monument.
You, you would never turn to stone.

What's behind you is a smiling shadow,
a voice in a room not meant for speaking.
You break your neck to look at me.

4

Let's move into rock and be what rocks become,
tooth on your tongue, chalk in your hand, dust.

Let's be nothing toward the ocean,
and then we'll be the ocean.

5

This poem is all precipice and gorge,
rim, switchback, edge, and sweat.

It says nothing
about a dimple of flesh

or the darkness of my body
which somehow contains my love for you.

6

There's something that lives beneath surfaces,
sometimes transparent,
sometimes blind with night or fog.

It has mood and electric shape.
We descend into it and rise from it
nourished and absent-minded.

It speaks through our bones
and out our mouths.
It is our love.

We're stranded in it,
swimming in it,
being held aloft by it.

It's been here
holding us
this whole time.

Your Poem to Me

is a bowl of roses swimming toward me
amidst a sea of books and your long drive
with the roses on your seat—but mostly
it's you seeing them in the first place, alive

to beauty and thinking of me. It's your
own hunger for time and space and the words
to live them in—your dark room, your closed door—
and still, there is green light. And still the birds

sing outside your window and you open
your arms to me and keep me. Your poem to me
is written every day, is a dozen
mangoes in a paper sack—only a few ripe.

Like your poem to me, the taste is sweet;
it's the knife to cut and the mouth to eat.

Seventeen Seconds on the Continental Divide

The fur of the bull elk rug
feels wrong beneath my feet
like stepping on forget-me-nots

here in the land of the ten thousand things.
Everything is a dedication to space and time,
each moment defined by fences and tree lines—

Come here, Come here, Come here,
the woman said, and I was there
with water rushing so hard

it pulled me by the throat. It was everything
I wanted to say, everything I meant.
I opened my mouth to speak,

but my body roared. In a dream, I stand
on the highest peak I can find,
and any step I might take is down.

The Continental Divide slivers
through me toward silver years,
and what is the remedy?

Catch a glacier snowball in July
in the thin air above DunRaven Pass,
and my skull pounds out a message

to make sure I know
the only way out is down.
Light scuds clouds with palest peach

and my heart beats fast and then slow again
and I can see a million miles into nowhere,
the horizon so far it's indeterminate.

The robins Marco Polo through the forest
beside our tent. Was that only yesterday
or the day before when ravens

left their prints and gifts
on our rental, when Old Faithful
spouted as soon as we walked up

as if in greeting. Someone said,
There she goes, and up she shot
like a goddess in a *Sinbad* movie—

chuffing and climbing a hundred feet up
to take a look around. An hour
and a half later, she does it again.

I read about pressure build-up
and chain reactions and felt sorry
for her... it's hard to be wired that way.

Or was that three or four days ago?
Thirteen hours of driving,
and the windshield is filthy.

Come back, Come back, Come back,
the child said, giving me
another part of the spell,

and I'm back: the Milky Way is a piece
of netting caught up in the trees
with Venus, Mars, and Saturn

lining up their own peak with the Rockies
to the West. Here at Yellowstone,
the caldera simmers and farts, boils

and belches superhot water crackling turquoise
and umber, living creatures in boiling pits
that reek of sulfur. In our tent

asleep between a volcano and a hail storm
that dents our coffee pot,
even the weather is saying, *Run away!*

But what comes next? What's the rest
of the spell? What's the progression?
Come here, Come back—then what?

Did we leave too soon? Will I ever know?
Intuition has yet to supply an answer.
I hope to know before we travel too far.

I've recorded every bird call, pebble,
and particle of water. The temperatures
fluctuate, attitude shifts by degrees

here and there. How can you trust
an avalanche? Is there any such thing
as a safe place? As soon as I saw

his sandals touch the blue-wet stone,
I turned away. I couldn't
bear to see the water sweep him away.

I saw him standing atop
his own highest peak, his own Divide,
determined like me to take

all new steps on the way down.
Come here, come back, they said,
and I'm five feet from a grizzly bear,

car window open, watching
through my camera lens a bear,
a real live mama grizzly bear

and her two cubs on the side of the road.
I had to tell myself the outcome hasn't happened yet,
anything could happen, anything at all.

I thought my heart might've beat a little harder,
like the time we had to brake hard on I-80,
I flew my pulse to the moon and back

and ended up having to dial myself down again,
back down to indeterminate
where I'll just look out this window

and let the road rock me
and the window turns into a music video
for the Cure's most perfect album.

Hello, Nebraska, I want to say.
Cheesier still, *Hello, America!*
Her onion trucks and giant windmills hail us.

I give up on trying to paint and let
the greens, blues, golds, and roses
shuttle through me like the water

down Avalanche Gorge, frothed white
at its most excited and insistent,
a wild and sweeping single thing,

blind and violent and primal.
We hike up the gorge belting bear songs
and clapping hands with one sky

made completely of rock. Below glacier melts,
three waterfalls descend in ribbons
to the stream where I leave my fear behind,

just let it evaporate in the water
so cold I stop caring the rocks are sharp.
I understand why the husband

went in after the wife
when she slipped from the bridge
into the raging river. What I want

to know is why she fell in the first place.
If I were a little crazier, I'd go myself
into the tumult and bruise, giant fists,

mindless arrival, the perfect way to go,
food for the fish and grizzlies. So why
should I worry? Avalanche Lake,

green palmful of glacier runoff,
lip of a body of water, holds
itself calm and still at the precipice

only to roar over the edge, eat rocks,
saying what the hell all the way down,
and 96 percent of me wants to join in

though the other four percent won't budge
and it's gotta be unanimous.
We hike back down the gorge

singing bear songs and clapping,
and I keep looking for ravens
or crows out the window, instead spot

dead coyote, raccoon, fox.
Deer graze among cattle.
I'm leaping from boulder to boulder...

was that seven days ago? Or nine?
At the northern-most point in Michigan,
Lake Superior is an inverted mountain of water,

and we're standing atop an unfurling
peninsula, frozen in rock-time,
foam on the crest, overfull

and spilling, hills hallowed
by copper. A quartz vein glitters
white through the weathered cliff

glowing agate. On the edge of nowhere,
orange, maroon, and lime-green lichen
dot boulders that would be lost

in the fog if they weren't solid
beneath my feet, where I kneel
in a hollow for a strawberry,

a perfect tiny fruit
beneath serrated leaves. Its naked
deep-rose roots cling to the cliff,

fog- and rock-fed,
a gathering of a gift
I pluck and eat, grind its seeds

between my teeth. It's sharper
than it is sweet, copper sandberry
on the edge of the indefinite,

a gift one must acknowledge.
The beach is all chert and spiders
and a thousand clicks with every ebbing wave.

I turn my back on the beyond,
try to mix red and yellow paint
to find an orange to match that lichen

that grows on the boulders.
You know, practical things...
potable water, Trio bars, leaving

a little blood and piss
for the waves to wash clean. It's one
of my last in a long line of bloodworks,

an animal clock that will soon
start stopping. We descend
the mountain, take turns driving

toward the hotter, the flatter,
the more common. Our landscapes
remain inside us, impossible

jutting and boiling earth, the birth
and descent of water filling
both gallon jugs we drank through

Nebraska. I return with Lake Superior
water in my paint jar,
pebbles in my pockets,

a husband who would come in after me,
and though the road winds beneath us,
we know it's taking us home.

Love Life

All along, the hand held in the dark,
the blurred edge, the flannel chest,

sun-warmed cotton, the neck and shoulders,
the hand on the wheel, the open path stare,

the *Why not?* the *What about now?*
the one through it all. The crosswords

and puzzles, our refusal to destroy
our messy castle and happy bed, our chores

and porridge, knit slippers, painted quilts,
hungry fireplace. Oak-leaf shadows above,

do you remember, on the tent ceiling pitched
behind the dune, the muted roar of the surf

against the wind caught in the leaves overhead,
sticks underfoot, underbed, the crunching give

of sand, real and touching us, napping, quiet.
All along, chipmunks bark, sparrows wait,

redstart demands, and we watch, listen,
you and me, holding hands, understood.

The Scream

It's taken me years to understand fusion.
Or is it fission? Or why I go nuclear. I mean,
why I seem to contain magma plumes

like a Scream's been happening inside me non-stop
since I was five years old, contained here in this human body
to be released only in moments of weakness.

When my dearest love speaks of enduring a Scream,
tears spring into his eyes like it's still happening.
I've seen his hair blow back like in a cartoon...

I see him see the wild animal in me,
when he is loving the Banshee in me,
when he has to grip the table to keep from falling over,

my Scream so deep and so true, pointed at him,
yes, but not meant for him, though he stands
amidst my roar the way someone might lash

themself to a palm tree during a hurricane
to better witness the primordial power of existence.
I see him see me. I see him forgive me

and love me and know me better now.
When it's over, he's as strong and brave
as the Universe itself. He tells me

that was a Diamond of a Scream,
a Milky Way Galaxy of a Scream, and inside it,
he opened his eyes. He was not afraid,

not enraged but loving me, curious, silent,
his head in the lion's mouth, staring straight into the face
of a child who lost all hope of ever being seen.

True Love

Clove, lilac,
vanilla, musk—

the odor unfolds
around me.

I think it's him,
something

he's put on
like that beard oil

I made for him.
I smile,

remember him
with a look on his face

like love is beaming
out of him so bright

it's all he can do
to hang on.

In the same moment,
he stops mid-step and turns

to show me the lily
blooming in the window.

That's how you know
it's love:

when we smell
a flower,

our first thought
is each other.

Twenty-forty-five

In 2045, blue will be indigo, orange will be rust,
and white will be linen. A cloud swirls
into fractals above an azure sea,
our boat, seaweed and maroon.

Palm fronds, third eyes, almond oil.
We'll carry the sun in a basket,
the moon in our hands,
the stars will confetti our pockets.

The world's cats will be our cats.

Wife will mean a flash of crimson in a crowd,
a billow of steam on an arid planet,
wet and white, a tongue-licked smile,
sandy skin, espresso eyes, silver hair.

Wife will mean the shadow of a leaf
against white sand
stark as a painting,
a taste of apple lingering.

Husband will mean 50-grit kisses,
a sunburned nose, the taste of sweat,
a quiet place for a thousand years, a nudge,
something in the lost and found no one claims.

Husband will mean mango and cinnamon,
sun falling slant on stacked rows of gold coins
on our window sill, things we never spend,
diamonds in our eyes, emeralds at our feet.

Every day is a car in the train to 2045
in a long line of days, cars that clack and roll,
they thunder and drum their fingers,
the lawn mowers, street corner guitars,

the soundtracks of our daily life.
An open window delivers grass, apple blossom,
sizzling meat vendors, hand woven rags,
the sort of sandal the natives wear.

Here we are on the first leg around the lake.
Here we are climbing the stairs, fingertips touching.
Here we emerge from a tunnel dazzled and blinking.
Our cargo is priceless,

this thing between our palms,
passed from my lips to yours and back to mine,
spent, replenished, renewed.
We're rich with cargo. We travel.

Great Love—for Scott

Bigger than the sum of its parts,
we weave this basket together,
a field of intention that surrounds us,

holds us in place while the universe
flings us about the galaxy. Inside,
we know ourselves to be loved.

Stack us one on top of the other to infinity
and you're close to the height of Great Love;
reach your arms around me

and we're nearing the capacity.
Let's hold hands into another day,
once again into the great unknown!

When I look at you, I see clean lines
and gentle curves somehow containing
your exotic, ferocious fire.

Great Love is our atomic fuel,
it's our hammock, our picnic table,
our cats stalking each other in the dark.

Great Love calls us lovers entwined
as we are in each other's gravity.
Great Love always fills the shape

of the space between us, fluid, fluent,
sometimes at a great distance,
never far apart. Sometimes

there's no space between us at all.
It's like we've known each other
since we were newborn stars

and our love burned the night,
as if we've always been everything,
buoyant, entangled, in love.

Now

The first smell of earth in Spring,
fallen leaves' sweet decay,
eat a tomato fresh from the vine.

Night and day, above and below,
outside and in, together apart,
the whole world divided, yet one.

Asleep, awake. Insignificant. Immense.
Wake to a sound, unafraid.
The power goes out in the shower—

I do not scream.
I don't even think about screaming.
It hits me later: I wasn't afraid.

Then I smile, a small secret smile.
All day long, my love returns my smile
when we pass each other shy in hallways.

The sun rises and the sun sets.
Every day is the same day.
Every moment is now.

Last Will and Testament

When you find the place to scatter my ashes,
make it somewhere to linger,
a place that pools and flows and pools again,

a place where each grain of me might
marry the terrain.
Drop me near the edge of that disappearing lake,

the one that reappears. Be sure the place
you scatter my ashes
has prospects for lightning strikes.

I'll believe in miracles if you scatter me
among pebbles
of granite, basalt, quartz, and fossil

evidence from the Devonian Age. A long hike
will take you to the place where
my ashes should be scattered,

marked on a canvas you know.
Feed me to that dune with purple
shadows lashed with wind and sun.

I want to be a cloud to glyph and scud
an ancient tongue across the sky.
Electric, I'll sing in crow, eagle, and wren.

Organic, I'll shiver your tongue
in berry's burst, sweet and sour sacrifice,
the only place I'd rather be.

Bring me to the dune by the lake
where I'll always be beautiful.
Give me away, my love. Scatter me free.

Acknowledgements and Thanks

3288 Review, "The Ascension of Joy" and "New Girl in Paradise"
Bitchn' Kitch, "Icarus as a Girl"
Big Windows Review, "Myth of the Perfect Girl"
Bitterzoet, "The Queen of Childhood"
Blue Lake Review, "Drunk Ages"
Charles Carter Review, "Sleeping Beauty Awakens"
The Dime Show Review, "The Enlightenment of Eve"
Earth's Daughters, "Everything is Magic" and "Incarnation"
Gordon Square Review, "Initiation" now called "The Secret Everyone Knows"
MacGuffin Michigan Poet Hunt, first place, "Still Life"
Nimrod: International Journal, "Dreaming Our Life"
The PrePress Awards, Volume Two: Michigan Voices, "Bloodstone and Agate"
Voices: first place adult division 1994 Dyer-Ives Poetry Competition, "Renovation"
Waxing and Waning, "Rock, Paper, Air"
YES Poetry, "Mother"

I want to thank the people who helped me make this book. Scott Krieger, Herb Scott, Nancy Eimers, John Woods, Lee Upton, Dan Gerber, Patricia Clark, Donna Munro, Neil Kaufman, Barbara Saunier, Matt Shade, and John Hunting. Also huge thanks to writing group members past and present, Toni Bal, Kim Bazzy, Pam Stephens, Sarah Klingenberg, Libby Sturrus, Molly Batchik, Lisa Gundry. I want to thank the Grand Rapids Poetry Community for being so awesome.
 —CMSK

Christine Stephens-Krieger (she/her) is the 8th Poet Laureate of Grand Rapids, Michigan (2024-2027). She has been active in the local poetry scene since the 1990s and has contributed many years of community work to celebrate local poets, including longtime coordination of the Dyer-Ives Poetry Competition and the creation of a project she fund-raised and produced called *An Oral History of Poetry in Grand Rapids*, which was delivered to the Grand Rapids Public Library Archives in 2024 (also on YouTube #OHPGR). Her current projects include The Grand River Poetry Collective (.com), which is concerned with publishing and creating a network where local poets can share skills and opportunities, as well as a poetry documentary called *Poetry is* Magic: *The Power of Poetry in Grand Rapids*. Christine graduated with a BA in English from GVSU and an MFA from WMU in Creative Writing with an emphasis in poetry. She's currently creating curriculum and teaching in the Frederik Meijer Honors College at GVSU and also teaches at Aquinas College. Christine is widely published in magazines and journals; she's won first place in the Dyer-Ives Poetry Competition and the MacGuffin Michigan Poet Hunt and was featured in the anthology, *PrePress Awards 2: Emerging Michigan Voices*. She currently lives in Grand Rapids with husband, author and poet Scott Krieger, and several fabulous cats.